INDEX

Born in 1995 under the authorship of Rasmus Lerdorf ,PHP or Hypertext Pre-processor is a programming language developed for web development *(But you already know that, don't you?)*.

This programming language has constantly changed, matured and been improved throughout the 20 years of it's life *(If you are reading in 2015)*.

PHP was initially created to support only structured programming, but as it has evolved, PHP has started offering complete support to Object Orientation, easing the development of Frameworks *(Group of tools that facilitates coding and allows writing cleaner code)* and CMS *(Content Management Systems)*, winning over a larger audience.

Nowadays it is estimated that there are over 240 million websites developed using PHP all over the world*, 60 million of these are using WordPress (A CMS developed in PHP), not to mention millions of Magento and Open Cart users, two e-commerce tools developed in PHP. The WordPress community alone has got 35 thousand plugins *(Part applications that add or modify the original functionality of a bigger application)*.

Using the .php extension and completely integrated to HTML, PHP became even more powerful as HTML developed and mixing with technologies such as CSS and JavaScript (and with that Query and Ajax).

In order to use PHP in the middle of HTML code, all that is needed are the tags <?php and ?>! It's support to different types of database allow data to be stored and managed, turning PHP into my favourite programming language. I'm pretty sure it is going to be your favourite too!

HOW TO START

Unlike HTML, where only your browser is required to see the magic happening, PHP requires a web server.

You can turn your own computer into a web server just by installing Apache and PHP afterwards, however I recommend installing WAMP *(In case you have got Windows)* or MAMP *(Should you use Macintosh)*. Both are easy to install packages that don't require any configuration and include both Apache and PHP as well as MySQL (Database). Either WAMP or MAMP are free and can be found on Google easily.

Although you can write PHP code even on notepad*, I recommend that you use an IDE such as Netbeans or Eclipse, however, for this book's purpose you can use something lighter like Notepad++ or PHP Editor, since both do not require any kind of configuration and are just as simple as notepad with several advantages like indentation and syntax highlighting that make coding easier. Once again, all of the above mentioned programs are free and can be found via Google.

USING A SERVER

Inside most web server's directory is a folder called "htdocs" or "www" and it's inside this folder that your PHP files should go. That being said, in order to access the server you need to go to "http://localhost/" using your browser, if the address does not work, the other possible address is "http://127.0.0.1".

I am not going to deeply detail how a web server works, since that is not this book's target, nevertheless, more information can be easily found on the internet. The same applies to how to use your server, regardless of the one you choose, more information will be available in great detail on it's web site.*

In addition, if a file called "test.php" is created inside the folders "www" or "htdocs", it can be seen by accessing the address: "http://localhost/test.php".

VARIABLES - PART I

"Memory allocation to store stuff", perhaps that is the simplest definition of variables. There are all kinds of types of variables for storing all different kinds of data *(Don't worry about that right now),* programmers used to other programming languages can find that weird, because in a strongly-typed language the variable type declaration is obligatory, for now just understand that PHP is taking care of that for you and will simply manage whatever variable type you want.

Therefore, if you need to store information for later use, you need to put it into a variable. Firstly the variable has to be named, *easy and intuitive names are highly recommended*, the second thing you going to need is the "=" operator, last but not least, you're going to need to include whatever you want to save! PHP's variables are preceded by "$", and nearly all code lines are ended with ";". Confusing? See the example:

```php
<?php
$variable = 1;
?>
```

In the above example, the number 1 is being stored into a variable called $variable.

There are some rules for naming variables, for instance, you cannot name a variable starting with numbers, yet you can use them anywhere else on the variable name.

Correct: $variable1

Wrong: $1variable

You can use capital letters, but remember, $variable is different to $Variable or to $VARIABLE, as variables are case sensitive You must not use special characters such as hash, quotation marks, etc. On the other hand, underscores can be used.

Now observe the following example:

```php
1  <?php
2  $variable = "1";
3  ?>
```

You will notice a subtle difference between the first example and the one above, however it may take you a minute to notice the difference. Below are both examples...

*See both examples now, line 2 is wrong and line 3 is right:**

```php
1  <?php
2  $variable_1 = this is an example;
3  $variable_2 = "this is an example";
4  ?>
```

Different to numbers, where having or not quotation marks will not make much of a difference in PHP, when working with strings, not having quotation marks will cause an error.

Know that variables are a temporary thing and that as soon as another page opens, it will be gone.

DEALING WITH FORMS

To illustrate below is a HTML form which I'm sure you've seen before, and below is how that form would look in a web browser

```
1    <form action="action.php" method="post">
2        <p>Type the first number:    <input type="text" name="number_1"/></p>
3        <p>Type the second number:   <input type="text" name="number_2"/></p>
4        <p><input type="submit"/></p>
5    </form>
```

Type the first number: [   ]

Type the second number: [   ]

[Submit]

On the first line of the above example, we have the most important HTML part. Where action is where the "target" is defined, or where the form data is going to be sent. So in other words, the file action.php will receive the typed numbers on the example fields. Method is where the form method is chosen to send the data to the file defined on action. For the purposes of this book, we will only consider the methods POST & GET.

Simply put, the difference between them is that GET will show the data on the URL and POST will not. When the submit button is hit using the method POST the url will be "action.php" whereas GET will be something like:

action.php?number_1=10&number_2=15

Notice that the number 10 was typed on the first field and 15 on the second.

We need to consider how we use that above mentioned 'action.php' to capture the form data. We are going to collect each input value and store each in a variable.

An interesting fact about variables is that PHP can generate some for you. An example are the variable called $_GET and $_POST. Every time you use the POST method in a PHP file, it will generate a $_POST variable for you and store all the data in it, the same applies when using the GET method.

See the below example, where number_1 from PHP's variable is saved in a custom built variable:

```php
1  <?php
2    $number_1 = $_POST["number_1"];
3  ?>
```

Please note that this variable is different to the ones we have seen so far, it has got brackets, quotation marks and a name in between, *don't worry about it right now, we will get there,* for now know only that all you need to do is change the text in between the quotation marks with the name in your HTML field.

An example of this is that if you had an input element with the name as 'test', we would use $_POST["test"]. This is the same principle for the $_GET method: $_GET["test"].

ECHO

Use the echo command to show content on your page. Say for instance we want to show data in the form of a number captured from a form like on the previous example that we looked at.

```php
1  <?php
2    $number_1 = $_POST["number_1"];
3    echo $number_1;
4  ?>
```

In the above example you will be collecting the number typed in a form, saving it in a variable and showing it on the screen. Similarly to storing numbers in variables, when storing a variable in another, you don't need quotation marks.

You can also mix text and variables without major problems when using quotation marks.

For instance, if you type the number 10 on the first field and use the following code:

```php
1  <?php
2    $number_1 = $_POST["number_1"];
3    echo "The typed number was $number_1";
4  ?>
```

You will get the following result:

The typed number was 10

However, if you use simple quotation marks:

```php
1  <?php
2    $number_1 = $_POST["number_1"];
3    echo 'The typed number was $number_1';
4  ?>
```

You will get:

The typed number was $number_1

Amongst other functions of the simple quotation marks, the most obvious is to allow typing things using $ preventing PHP from "thinking" it refers to a variable. Should you need to use a variable and simple quotation marks at the same time, you can always use concatenation. To concatenate, means put two things or more together, concatenation in PHP is made by using ".", as an example:

```
1   <?php
2       $number_1 = $_POST["number_1"];
3       echo 'The typed number was ' . $number_1;
4   ?>
```

The above code will result in:

The typed number was 10

Echo always supports HTML code, in such case the use of simple quotation marks can be very useful, as shown on the following example:

```
1   <?php
2       $number_1 = $_POST["number_1"];
3       echo 'The typed number was <font color="red">' . $number_1 . '</font>';
4   ?>
```

Which results in:

The typed number was 10

You can achieve the same result below using a slightly different method.

```
1   <?php $number_1 = $_POST["number_1"]; ?>
2   The typed number was <font color="red"><?php echo $number_1;?></font>
```

The result would be the exact same, but the code above is much easier to read. Another alternative would be the following code:

```
1    <?php $number_1 = $_POST["number_1"]; ?>
2    The typed number was <font color="red"><?= $number_1;?></font>
```

The short tag <?= can replace <?php echo and make your code even cleaner, even though the use of <?= is seen as controversial!

Except in some cases, as a general rule it is always more organised to separate HTML as much as possible from PHP, it is a good practice to separate these!

VARIABLES - PART II

As per previously mentioned, there are several types of variable, but that isn't something we need to concern ourselves with just yet., However we should consider a type of variable called an array,, these are slightly different to the other types of variables. We'll look at arrays in a little more detail.

A way of seeing an array is to think about them in terms of a lists. An array can store several types of data. Do you remember $_POST and $_GET? In reality they are associative arrays *(We will get there, I promise! :))*.

Say we need to list all the cars that a given client can buy in an application, all we need to do is:

```php
<?php
$cars = array("Celica", "New Civic", "Golf");
?>
```

Now let's say you need to show the first element of this array on the screen:

```php
<?php
$cars = array("Celica", "New Civic", "Golf");
echo $cars[0];
?>
```

Yes, the first element is 0 instead of 1, the second is 1 instead of 2 and so on.

Now say we want to store the car manufacturer as well, so that we can identify the cars by its manufactures. We would need associative array just like $_GET and $_POST, that identify the fields sent. Remember the example $_POST["number_1"]? See the example:

```php
1  <?php
2  $cars = array("Toyota"=>"Celica",
3                "Honda"=>"New Civic",
4                "Volkswagen"=>"Golf");
5  echo $cars["Honda"];
6  ?>
```

On the above example, the result will be:

New Civic

That way it is possible to show cars by using its manufacturer as the identifier instead of numbers.

The identifiers should be unique otherwise this will break our application. *Wait for the next bat-chapters, on the same bat-book.*

MATH OPERATORS

Returning to the two numbers example, it can be used for various mathematical operations. *I hope you have that code in hand! Otherwise have a quick glance at the "Dealing with forms" chapter.*

The math operators in PHP are + for adding, - for subtracting * for multiplying and / for dividing.

With the knowledge you have acquired at this stage, you should be able to perfectly understand the code below. If you have trouble understanding, it is recommended that you review the previous chapters about forms, variables and echo!

```php
1  <?php
2  $number_1 = $_POST["number_1"];
3  $number_2 = $_POST["number_2"];
4
5  $sum = $number_1 + $number_2;
6  ?>
7
8  <p>The first number typed was <font color="red"><?=$number_1;?></font></p>
9  <p>The second number typed was <font color="red"><?=$number_2;?></font></p>
10 <p>The sum of them results in <font color="red"><?=$sum;?></font></p>
```

In a scenario where the first number is 10 and the second is 5, the result for the above code will be:

The first number typed was 10

The second number typed was 5

The sum of the typed number is 15

Now try changing the sum sign for the other operators and see the obtained results, it's fun!

Ok not that much.

The code of the previous example is bigger than the one that we have looked at so far and can scare in the beginning, but you have enough knowledge to turn it into a smaller code. *And maybe confusing, but perfectly correct.*

Observe the example:

```
1   <p>The first number typed was <b><?= $_POST["number_1"];?></b>
2       and the second number was <b><?= $_POST["number_2"];?></b>
3       and their sum resulted in <b><?= $_POST["sum"];?></b></p>
```

Take some time to observe the above code and try to fully understand it. Remember, you have enough knowledge to understand it, if you need to revise any previous material, do not hesitate!

It is important to know that you are not limited to making one calculation per line, you may want to do something like this:

($numero_1 + $numero_2) * $numero_1.

The parenthesis on the example has the same mathematical function as in maths, in such case the sum will be prioritised. Just like in maths, the multiplication usually takes priority over other operations unless there is a parenthesis telling otherwise.

CONDITIONS

Time to provide logic!

Conditions allow you to give logic to the code, thanks to a combination of logical operators, if, else, else if and switch, the sky is the limit! *I recommend you go through this chaper in one go, , so if you don't have time to read it all, it is probably best that you rest and come back later!*

COMPARISON OPERATORS

First, have a good look at the comparison operators, the most important ones are:

- **==** Equals to
- **>** Greater than
- **<** Less than
- **>=** Greater than or equal to
- **<=** Less than or equal to
- **!=** Not equal to

They don't have much power alone, however, when combined with conditional statements, they are very powerful. It is worth highlighting that there is a huge difference between "=" *(Which has got the function of setting value to something)* and "==" *(Which compares two things)*.

IF

Maybe the most important thing that you will learn and barely has no change across various programming languages is the conditional If.

I believe that the most effective way of learning the If is to explain it and show its functionality while showing a working example. Observe the following example which also uses the fields number_1 and number_2:

```php
1   <?php
2   $number_1 = $_POST["number_1"];
3   $number_2 = $_POST["number_2"];
4   $result = 0;
5
6   if ($number_1 > $number_2){
7       $result = $number_1 + $number_2;
8   }
9
10  echo $result;
11  ?>
```

The lines 2, 3 and 4 don't bring anything new, the values from $_POST are set to variables. On line 6, we ought to read:

If variable number_1 is greater than variable number_2, do.

Everything in between brackets, will be executed should the condition is met, otherwise PHP will ignore the block completely and will not execute a thing.

On line 10 it is shown the value of the variable $result which was previously set. However, what would happen when the condition is not met? *0 is shown, since the value was set prior to the condition.*

Setting 0 to the variable $result before the condition, guarantees that it will exist when echoing it, avoiding errors. In case the condition is not met, 0 will be shown.

ELSE

The else can be extremely handy when it comes to more complex conditions. See the example below...:

```php
1   <?php
2       $number_1 = $_POST["number_1"];
3       $number_2 = $_POST["number_2"];
4
5       if ($number_1 > $number_2){
6           $result = $number_1 - $number_2;
7       }
8
9       if ($number_1 <= $number_2){
10          $result = $number_1 + $number_2;
11      }
12
13      echo $result;
14  ?>
```

Don't get overwhelmed with the size of the code, soon enough you will get used to working with more complicated code.

Note that this time the variable $result isn't set before the condition, when PHP reaches the echo, $result will always be set, one way or another! Let's read line 5 and line 9, respectively:

If variable number_1 is greater than variable number_2, do:

If variable number_1 is less or equal to variable number_2, do:

To cut a long story short, if $number_1 is greater than $number_2, they are going to be subtracted, in case they are less or equal they are going to be summed. See? It does not matter what happens, the $result will always be set, but you must agree that the below code is much smarter and simple:

```php
1   <?php
2   $number_1 = $_POST["number_1"];
3   $number_2 = $_POST["number_2"];
4
5   if ($number_1 > $number_2){
6       $result = $number_1 - $number_2;
7   }else{
8       $result = $number_1 + $number_2;
9   }
10
11  echo $result;
12  ?>
```

We can achieve the same result with less code, see lines 5 and 7:

If variable number_1 is greater than variable number_2, do.

If not, do.

ELSE IF

The else if is a fusion of else with if and allows to insert more than one condition to the same logic. For instance:

```php
1   <?php
2   $number_1 = $_POST["number_1"];
3   $number_2 = $_POST["number_2"];
4
5   if ($number_1 > $number_2){
6       $result = $number_1 - $number_2;
7   }else if ($number_1 == $number_2){
8       $result = $number_1 + $number_2;
9   }else
10      $result = $number_1 * $number_2;
11  }
12
13  echo $result;
14  ?>
```

In the previous example, lines 5, 7 and 9 are read as follows, respectively:

If variable number_1 is greater than variable number_2, do.

If not and if variable number_1 equals to variable number_2, do.

If not one of the above is met, do.

In short, in case $number_1 is greater than $number_2, the first block will be executed, in case $number_1 is equal to $number_2 the second block will be executed, in case none of the conditions are met, and in this case only if $number_1 is greater than $number_2, the third block will be executed.

LOGICAL OPERATORS

The logical operators give even more power to the conditionals, for the purposes of this books, only the OR and the AND matter. Their use will be seen just below through practical examples.

MULTIPLE COMPARISONS AND COMMENTS

The If statement also can be used to compare more than one item, and that is why the logical operators are so powerful.

The following example, of a hypothetical form which has one field called age, shows an excellent representation of the use of the logical operator and:

```php
1   <?php
2       // receives age
3       $age = $_POST["age"];
4
5       // age less than 16
6   if ( $age < 16 ){
7           echo "Voting is not allowed";
8       }
9       // age greater than or equal to 16 and less than 18
10  if (( $age >= 16 ) and ( $age < 18 )){
11          echo "Voting is optional";
12      }
13      // age greater than or equal to 18 and less than 65
14  if (( $age >= 18 ) and ( $age < 65 )){
15          echo "Voting is an obligation";
16      }
17      // age greater than or equal to 18 and less than 65
18  if ( $age >= 65 ){
19          echo "Voting is exempted";
20      }
21  ?>
```

On the previous example, a simple program that decides whether you're obligated to vote in Brazil or not, and is used for executing multiple comparisons twice, first to verify if the age was greater or equal to 16 and *also* less than 18. And afterwards, on line 14 to verify whether the age was greater or equal to 18 and less than 65.

Note that in multiple conditions, each condition was isolated in its own parenthesis and both surrounded by parenthesis. *I personally find it much more organised that way.*

Note on the example that we have some pieces of text in grey that have // in front of them, these are comments. Comments in general are used as a way of organisation so that you know what is going on on a piece of code with a quick glance at the code.

Comments are not read by PHP, they are completely ignored. The use of // is one way the various ways of commenting the code.

Now let's have a look at an example of or, on a similar form, only now we want the system to inform just whether the person is obligated to vote in Brazil or not, no additional information whatsoever. Check it out:

```php
1   <?php
2       // receives age
3       $age = $_POST["age"];
4
5       // age less than 18 or greater than / equal to 65
6       if (( $age < 18 ) or ( $age >= 65 )){
7           echo "Voting is not an obligation";
8       }else{
9           echo "Voting is an obligation"
10      }
11  ?>
```

Incredible simple, isn't it? Practice makes perfect.

Although this book's examples don't have more than two conditions per If statement, you can have as many as you need. You can also nest one inside another. *Before proceeding to Switch I strongly recommend reading If from the beginning at least once again.*

SWITCH

Once you have recovered from the brain damage caused by the previous example, keep on reading.

Depending on the amount of items to be considered, the If by itself or a mix with else if may turn into something confusing. In theory every time that If turns into something misleading or confusing, and the comparisons are only for checking whether something equals to another something, it is highly recommended using Switch.

See the example where user names are sent through a field called username:

```php
1   <?php
2   $username = $_POST["username"];
3
4   switch ( $username ){
5       case "edward":
6           echo "Administrator";
7           break;
8       case "john":
9           echo "user";
10          break;
11      case "michael":
12          echo "user";
13          break;
14      default:
15          echo "Not found";
16  }
17  ?>
```

The switch indicates the target for the comparison, in this case, the variable $username. Line 5 is read like this:

In case $username is edward

Incase the conditions are met, the whole block of code in between the colon and the break, will be executed. Apart from very specific situations (which we will not exemplify here) the break must be used at all times. There is no need to use break on the default default block. The default block is the one executed when none of the conditions are met, on the given example, every time neither "eduardo" nor "john" nor "michael" is typed

You just finished the most important chapter of the book, congratulations! All you've learnt so far needs to be clear in your head, since now we're going to move forward to subjects that will use examples that require everything we learnt so far.

Review as many times needed before proceeding, however just reviewing this chapter may be not enough, try reproducing the examples given in this book by copying and remaking them yourself and then try creating challenges, increasing the difficulty as you go.

FUNCTIONS - PART I

In short, function in PHP is a code to execute another piece of code. *Confusing?* You must have noticed that the code we have seen so far are executed line by line, from top to bottom, from the first line to the last. If the code has a function, we can change that order, execute from the middle to end, from the beginning jump to end and etc... *Confusing?* Basically functions are divided in two parts, the creation and its summon/execution, wherein the second part can be done endless times. We will go in further details on that later, for now just keep this abstract knowledge in mind and remember that functions are extremely useful and that every function you execute in your code has to be previously created, and sometimes not by you. *Even more confused?*

f you are asking yourself why would want to change the order of you code, putting the beginning in the end and vice versa, it is not like that. The big advantage of the functions as previously mentioned is thatthey can be executed multiple times. For instance, say you have a piece of your code that is used a couple of times, it would be a smart decision and good practice to create a function and call it twice (or as many time as you need). *In case you are feeling your brain melting at this point, take a break, have a coffee and don't worry, we won't go into too much details just yet.*

The fact that the very same code can be executed several times facilitates also the code distribution, letting programmers codify classic routines that most programmers need and sharing on the internet, that way other programmers only need to call the function without having to code it himself.

Taking advantage of that, PHP has got hundreds of native functions so that you don't you have to create in your code, but that are available for use.

The normal behaviour of a function follows the following order: Receive data, process it and return a result.

Enough of the theory.

Imagine a HTML form with a field called "name" which sends data through the post method to a PHP page, check the example:

```php
<?php
$name = $_POST["name"];
$quantityOfLetters = strlen( $name );
echo "You name's got $quantityOfLetters letters";
?>
```

The native function strlen counts characters. Notice that the function was not created at any moment. Also notice that the content to be process was sent in between the parentheses that follow the function's name, and that's call you execute/call/summon a function. Don't worry just now if you didn't fully understand, we will have a look at other examples.

The above code also could have had been represented this way:

```php
<?php
$name = $_POST["name"];
echo "You name's got " . strlen( $name ) . " letters";
?>
```

Or even:

```
1   <?php
2     echo "You name's got " . strlen( $_POST["name"] ) . " letters";
3   ?>
```

In all cases, if the name was "Eduardo", we would obtain the below result:

Your name has got 7 letters

There are no limitations on what you can do with the result of a function, for instance, you don't need to echo it, you could do something like the following example:

```
1   <?php
2   if ( strlen( $_POST["name"] ) > 5 ){
3       echo "Your name's got more than 5 characters, cool."
4   }else{
5       echo "You have such short name";
6   }
7   ?>
```

That way we check if the name has got more than 5 characters, we do something with it.

SOME USEFUL FUNCTIONS AND EXAMPLES

strtolower() Turns all the letters into lowercase.

strtoupper() Capitalises all the letters.

Both examples are used in a similar way to the strlen, providing a parameter in between parentheses and getting a result. Example:

```
1   <?php
2     echo strtoupper( $_POST["name"] );
3   ?>
```

Should the sent value were "Eduardo", the result would be:

date() Shows the current date, but needs information about the desired result. In case the result wanted is something like "31/05/1991", the code would be:

```
1  <?php
2    echo date("d/m/Y");
3  ?>
```

For further details on how to use date, visit: http://php.net/manual/en/function.date.php

Moreover, PHP.net owns a list of all the PHP native functions, as well as the documentation on how to use them. Every time you're in doubt, go check the website and you will most likely find an answer!

Now let's see an example of a function which receives 3 parameters instead of 1, **str_replace()**:

```
1  <?php
2    $browser = "The best browser is Firefox";
3    $browser = str_replace("Firefox", "Chrome", $browser);
4    echo $browser;
5  ?>
```

The function str_replace searches for a value and overwrites it. The first parameter to be sent is the one to be searched, the second will be the substitute and the third is the place to search. On the above example the result would be:

The best browser is Chrome

I don't intend to bombard you with lots of useful functions, but that you will most likely forget in five minutes or so. On the

contrary, I want you to clear your mind, because you are about to burn all your neurones understanding loops! Will be back to the subject shortly and some other functions will be introduced throughout the book.

LOOPS

For, Foreach and While, are the three types of loop we will be studying, all of them have the role of running the same piece of code several times, nevertheless each of them has its own uses.

FOR

The For is normally used when we have control over how many times the piece of code must be executed

For divides itself in 3 pieces, the first where the counter is started, the second where the logic is tested, finishing or continuing the loop and the third where the counter is increased (or decreased).

In the example below, the counter is started at 1, to do so the variable $i is used. You could have given $i any start number. Afterwards the logic is tested to check whether the variable is less than or equal to 10, and in case the logic test passes the code will be executed. If the code is not equal to 10 the code stops executing. At last +1 is increased to the variable. *Here we have everything you have learned so far and used on the For, except for the $i++, which is the same as $i=$i+1.*

```php
1   <?php
2   for ( $i = 1; $i <= 10; $i++ ){
3       echo $i;
4   }
5   ?>
```

The result of the above code is:

12345678910

In short the loop was executed until the condition was not met anymore, in other words when $i turned 11, the code stopped executing.

Too hard? Challenge yourself and try to write a code that will execute all the even numbers up to 20, having each number in a separated line, without looking at the below example! If you get it all right, it means you understood it all perfectly, should you run into any trouble have a quick look at the code below:

```php
1  <?php
2  for ( $i = 1; $i <= 20; $i = $i+2 ){
3      echo $i . "<br/>";
4  }
5  ?>
```

The result for the above script is:

1
3
5
7
9
11
13
15
17
19

On the code above the variable started at 1, the code was executed while the variable was less than 20, and every time it executed 2 was added to $i, that way since we started with an even number, only even numbers were obtained until the end. *If you did it alone, congratulations!*

Bonus: The same way that "++" adds 1 to a variable, "--" reduces 1. In summary, the same way that $i++ equals to $i = $i + 1, $i—is also equals to $i = $i – 1.

FOREACH

Foreach runs through every item of an array and executes a piece of code whilst doing it.

```php
1  <?php
2      $cars = array("Celica", "New Civic", "Golf");
3
4  foreach ( $cars as $car ){
5          echo ($car . "<br/>");
6  }
7  ?>
```

On the above example the result obtained is:

Celica

New   Civic

Golf

Foreach needs just 2 parameters, the first needs to be an array, the second any variable. The value of the second parameter will change every time the piece of code is executed and the array ran. For instance, on the above array, the first time the Foreach executes, the variable $car will receive "Celica", the second "New Civic" and at last "Golf".

When you need to list items of an array, most of the times foreach will be your best bet.

WHILE

Similarly to For, While also verifies when a determined action and only continues when it is true. See the following example:

```php
1  <?php
2  $validator = "";
3  $counter = 1;
4  while ( $validator != "12345" ){
5      $validator = $validator . $counter;
6      echo "The counter is at $counter";
7      echo "The validator equals to $validator";
8      $counter++;
9  }
10 ?>
```

The result of the below example is:

The counter equals 1 The validator equals to 1
The counter equals 2 The validator equals to 12
The counter equals 3 The validator equals to 123
The counter equals 4 The validator equals to 1234
The counter equals 5 The validator equals to 12345

Technically the example does not have any useful functionality, it however exemplifies very well the use of While.Notice the code inside the loop was executed until the moment that the conditions was no longer met ($validator equals 12345).

Before proceeding it's important that you have understood the concept of loops, it doesn't matter if you can't really use it just yet or comprehend its usefulness, since you have plenty of other examples throughout the next chapters, but it's crucial that the concept and the differences between the types are fully understood.

VARIABLES – PART III

Until now we've only looked at arrays with one dimension, however they can have unlimited dimensions. n the last example of arrays, an array containing several car branches, imagine a scenario where a variable needs to store also the car's technical specifications.

Observe:

```
1  <?php
2  $cars = array("Celica"      => array("Engine 2.0", "6 gears"),
3                "New Civic"   => array("Engine 1.8", "5 gears"),
4                "Golf"        => array("Engine 1.6", "5 gears"));
5  ?>
```

On the above example there is an array inside the other. You can have an array inside the other and that array may contain another and so on so forth as long as it's convenient. The example above can be overwritten by the bellow:

```
1  <?php
2  $cars = array("Celica", "New Civic", "Golf" );
3  $cars[0] = array("Engine 2.0", "6 gears");
4  $cars[1] = array("Engine 1.8", "5 gears");
5  $cars[2] = array("Engine 1.6", "5 gears");
6  ?>
```

Using the previously learnt, foreach, we can "walk through" the array and easily list it.

As the example has got two layers of array, the car models will become array keys, and slightly changing the foreach, we can access them too, see the full example:

```php
1   <?php
2   $cars = array("Celica"     => array("Engine 2.0", "6 gears"),
3                 "New Civic"  => array("Engine 1.8", "5 gears"),
4                 "Golf"       => array("Engine 1.6", "5 gears"));
5
6   foreach ( $cars as $key=>$car ){
7       echo "<b>" . $key . "</b><br/>";
8       foreach ( $car as $description ){
9           echo $description . "<br/>";
10      }
11  }
12  ?>
```

Notice that were needed two foreach statements, one for each layer.
The above example shows the following result:

Celica

2.0 Engine

6 Gears

New Civic

1.8 Engine

5 Gears

Golf

1.6 Engine

5 Gears

Working with several array layers can be tough, I recommend reading this chapter over and over again and some practicing before proceeding to the next. Make some changes on the example and make some tests with it to clear possible doubts.

FUNCTIONS – PART II

Previously, the functions were explained and shown, *and it's very important the concept is fully understood before you continue*, now we will learn how to create our own functions. As per good practice, a function must be created every time a code needs to execute more than once.

In this part of the explanation, beginners tend to confuse the concept of function and a loop which is something completely different.

A loop executes a piece of code repeatedly at once, whilst a function executes a piece of code that can be repeated throughout the software – including inside the function itself – on big softwares, the same code can be executed several times in different occasions..

You can use any code inside a function, including other functions, loops, conditions and as we've mentioned previously, even the function itself. The act of calling a function inside itself is called recursion, we won't get any deeper on the subject, but it's always good to know.

It's also important to say that what happens inside a function stays inside (just like Vegas) until told otherwise. You can even use variable names that are being used in other parts of the code because the variables won't be sharing or losing any data.

For the first example, we will create a function that will execute mathematical operations using two numbers, according to the user's input.

```php
1   <?php
2     echo calculate(10, 15, "sum");
3     echo "<br/>";
4     echo calculate(1, 2, "sum");
5     echo "<br/>";
6     echo calculate(12, 2, "subtract");
7
8     function calculate( $number1, $number2, $action ){
9         if ( $action == "sum" ){
10            $result = $number1 + $number2;
11        }else ( $action == "subtract"){
12            $result = $number1 - $number2;
13        }else{
14            $result = "Operation not supported";
15        }
16        return $result;
17    }
18  ?>
```

The result for the code above is:

25
3
10

In order to create a function, it's used function and its name of the function comes following. The chosen name is the same that will be typed in order to call it.

Above was constructed a function named calculate, that supports 3 parameters. In this case, **in order for the function to work,** it needs 3 parameters, if no parameter is sent or the wrong number is sent, PHP will find an error and will stop the execution.

The code return makes sure $result comes out of the function, going to the original scope of the program, without it nothing would be produced by the function and $result would be lost forever.

Observe the next example:

```php
1   <?php
2   $res1 = calculate(2, 0);
3   $res2 = calculate(4, 2, "sum");
4   $res3 = calculate(3, 1, "subtract");
5
6   function calculate( $number1, $number2, $action="sum" ){
7       if ( $action == "sum" ){
8           $result = $number1 + $number2;
9       }else ( $action == "subtract"){
10          $result = $number1 - $number2;
11      }else{
12          $result = "Operation not supported";
13      }
14      return $result;
15  }
16  ?>
```

On this example, the result of calculate was store into different variables and shown afterwards. The result is:

2

6

2

It is also worth highlighting that the third parameter has become arbitrary. With the slight change made on the function creation, now every time the function is called without the third parameter it will automatically be set to "sum", if a parameter is sent, it will be used normally.

INCLUDES

When the code complexity is expanded, separating the code in smaller pieces is a great idea, each part taking responsibility for a determined "piece" of the software.

A good way of dividing is dividing in different files, each file storing a piece of the code that shapes the software. But in order to do that, it's necessary to put these files together somehow, and that's what include does.

The include syntax is simple, see:

```php
1  <?php
2    include ("myFunctions.php");
3  ?>
```

The above example can be used in a program where the main code is in one file and its functions are in another. In a small program, this kind of organisation is perfect, however in order to keep it all tidy and organised, much more files and maybe folders are needed when building big softwares.

SESSIONS

At the end of this chapter you will be able to create a login system, allowing you to create dashboard and restrict its access to logged users only, that most common way to do it is by using sessions.

Sessions allow data to be saved for future utilization. The data will continue to be available even after the file where the values are, is closed and another page opens, the user can close and open the browser or go to another website and it will still be available.

Sessions are not shared among browsers, meaning that a session available on Chrome will not be available on Firefox, and they will only be available for a limited amount of time that as per standard is 20 minutes.

SESSION_START()

The code session_start() has to be at the top of every page in what you want to use sessions, putting it anywhere else on the file can cause undesirable problems though it may work sometimes.

$_SESSION

Similarly to $_GET and to $_POST, $_SESSION also is an array. You can create a key and save any data in it, and this data will be available then. If used without session_start(), it won't return anything, even if you have had previously saved something on a session. *Don't worry, an example is coming...*

SESSION_DESTROY()

Deletes all the information stored in session. Just like anything else that relates to sessions, it needs to be used after session_start();

EXAMPLE – LOGIN AND LOGOUT

Although it's recommended that you type the code for memorisation purposes, the files will be available for download at:

http://www.eduardoleoni.com.br/files/livro_login_com_sessions_exemplo.zip

If for some reason you are not able to put the program together just by copying from the book, download this file and compare to your code to look for the error.

This example is much bigger than the others, challenge yourself and try to fully grasp understand it!

Start by creating the file functions.php which stores the following code:

```php
1   <?php
2   function checkIfLogged(){
3       if (isset( $_SESSION["username"] )){
4           return true;
5       }else{
6           return false;
7       }
8   }
9
10  function validateCredentials( $username, $password ){
11      if (( $username == "admin" ) && ( $password == "123456" )){
12          return true;
13      }else{
14          return false;
15      }
16  }
17
18  function login ( $username, $password ){
19      $validate = validateCredentials( $username, $password );
20      $if ( $validate == true ){
21          $_SESSION["username"] = $username;
22          return true;
23      }else{
24          return false;
25      }
26  }
```

This file stores functions that will be used by the program, they were named in a way that aims to ease the understanding and to allow guessing what the function does just by reading its name.

Except for the isset, you should be able to understand the whole code above. The isset finds out whether a variable exists or not, if the returned result is true, it means it does exist, should it be false, the variable doesn't exist.

The function checkIfLogged() makes good use of the isset, in case $_SESSION["user"] exists, that means the user is logged in the system. In $_SESSION["user"] is where the user will be stored, as will be seen soon. The function returns true in case the user is logged and false should he isn't.

The function validateCredentials() verifies if the system admin credentials are correct, returning true if they are and false should they aren't. For this example, the credentials will be as follows:

username: admin

password: 123456

login() will be responsible for calling validateCredentiais() in order to verify if the login details provided are valid and only after that fills $_SESSION["username"] with the user name. The function will return true in case the login succeeds and false if it fails.

Now create a file named as index.php and store the following code in it:

```php
1    <?php
2    session_start();
3    include("functions.php");
4    ?>
5    <html>
6        <head>
7            <meta charset="UTF-8">
8            <title></title>
9        </head>
10       <body>
11           <?php
12           if( checkIfLogged() == true ){
13           ?>
14               <p><b>Welcome <?php echo $_SESSION["username"];?>,</b></p>
15               <p><a href="dashboard.php">Go to your dashboard</a></p>
16               <p><a href="logout.php">Logout</a></p>
17           <?php
18           }elseif{
19               if( isset( $_POST["username"] ) == true ){
20                   $login = login( $_POST["username"], $_POST["password"]);
21                   if ( $login == true ){
22                       echo "You logged in successfully,
23                           click <a href = 'dashboard.php'>here</a>
24                           to go to your dashboard";
25                   }else{
26                       echo "Invalid username or password";
27                   }
28               }else{
29                   ?>
30                   <form method="post">
31                       <p>Username: <input type="text" name="username"/></p>
32                       <p>Password: <input type="text" name="password"/></p>
33                       <p>Username: <input type="submit" value="enter"/></p>
34                   </form>
35                   <?php
36               }
37           }
38           ?>
39       </body>
40   </html>
```

The above file first checks if the user is logged, in case he is he will have a welcome screen using a function previously written, the user name will also be shown, we have it on a session, since every time a user logs in, this information is stored in a session.

If the user is not logged, the system will check if the POST method is being used, if it is, that means the user is trying to log in and therefore we should validate its data and if they are valid the user will log into the system, if not a message should appear on the screen.

If the POST method is not being used and the user is not logged in, it means the login form should appear so that the user can log in…

Usually each of these things are stored in individual files, but to help you understand the example is shown this way. An excellent exercise is to separate each part described above afterwards. Remember, you have enough knowledge by now!

Observe the code for the file dashboard.php which is available after the user logs in:

```php
1   <?php
2   session_start();
3   include("functions.php");
4   ?>
5   <html>
6       <head>
7           <meta charset="UTF-8">
8           <title></title>
9       </head>
10      <body>
11          <?php
12          if ( checkIfLogged() == true ){
13          ?>
14              <p>
15                  <b>Welcome <?php echo $_SESSION["username"];?>,</b>
16                  <a href="logout.php">Logout</a>
17              </p>
18              <p>
19                  Lorem ipsum dolor sit amet, consectetur adipiscing elit.
20                  Proin suscipit commodo nibh eu volutpat. Suspendisse
21                  et rhoncus urna. Aenean mattis ipsum ac ullamcorper
22                  auctor. Integer id turpis tempus, pulvinar justo et,
23                  tincidunt metus. Pellentesque finibus congue turpis.
24                  Vivamus imperdiet congue pretium. Maecenas nec mi
25                  fringilla, euismod neque et, faucibus orci. Integer
26                  eu justo porttitor mauris fermentum pulvinar non vitae
27                  risus. Donec ultrices turpis vel ex lacinia, et vestibulum
28                  arcu tincidunt
29              </p>
30              <p>
31                  Lorem ipsum dolor sit amet, consectetur adipiscing elit.
32                  Proin suscipit commodo nibh eu volutpat. Suspendisse
33                  et rhoncus urna. Aenean mattis ipsum ac ullamcorper
34                  auctor. Integer id turpis tempus, pulvinar justo et,
35                  tincidunt metus. Pellentesque finibus congue turpis.
36                  Vivamus imperdiet congue pretium. Maecenas nec mi
37                  fringilla, euismod neque et, faucibus orci. Integer
38                  eu justo porttitor mauris fermentum pulvinar non vitae
39                  risus. Donec ultrices turpis vel ex lacinia, et vestibulum
40                  arcu tincidunt
41              </p>
42              <?php
43          }else{
44          ?>
45              <p style="color: red">
46                  You've no permission to view this content
47              </p>
48              <?php
49          }
50          ?>
51      </body>
52  </html>
```

Even though the above described file is relatively large, I hope you notice that the most part of it is formed by sample paragraphs.

The most important part is the condition that checks if the user has permission or not to view the file. The function checkIfLogged returns true if the user is logged in and thanks to that, everything that is inside this function only will be executed for logged users.

In case the user is not logged in, a message informing that the page is restrict will pop up.

By using this page as an example you can create several other exclusive functions for registered users, like alter its own password or execute an exclusive function of your website. Your creativity is the only limit here.

This page also gives the user the possibility of logging out.

The code for the logout.php file is seen just below.

```php
1   <?php
2     session_start();
3     include("functions.php");
4   ?>
5   <html>
6       <head>
7           <meta charset="UTF-8">
8           <title></title>
9       </head>
10      <body>
11          <?php
12          if ( checkIfLogged() == true ){
13              session_destroy();
14          ?>
15              <p>
16                  You logged out, click <a href - "index.php">here</a>
17                  to go back to the homepage.
18              </p>
19
20          <?php
21          }else{
22          ?>
23              <p>
24                  An error just happened click
25                  <a href - "index.php">here</a> to go back to
26                  the homepage.
27              </p>
28          <?php
29          }
30          ?>
31      </body>
32  </html>
```

This file checks if the user is logged in, in case it is, destroys the session and shows a success message. In case the user isn't logged in and trying to log out anyways, an error message will pop up.

I recommend that you modify these files as much as you can and try to apply all the knowledge acquired so far in order to practice and memorise everything. Challenge yourself!

DATABASES

This book doesn't aim to go deep into teaching databases or SQL, however, the reader will have sufficient proficiency on database to execute basic operations such as insert, delete and update rows in a table as well as execute tasks on previously created databases.

None of the above words makes sense to you or only some of them make sense? Keep on reading, however if you are familiar with the basic concepts of a database, don't waste your time and go straight to the subchapter "PHPMyAdmin".

Generically speaking, databases made of tables that are made of columns and rows, in a very superficial description, a column is very similar to a spreadsheet.

Picturing a database that manages a company, examples of tables would be: employees, sectors, open_positions...

Databases, tables and columns must be named without special characters and usually on lower case, just like on the above example "open_positions" rather than "Open Positions".

Columns examples for the employees table could be "name", "date_of_birth" and "salary". It's a good practice to have a column called "id" as primary key.

A very superficial explanation for primary keys is to say that they serve as connections to other tables. For instance, if the table "departments" had a column "id", the table "employees" could have a column called "department_id", that way we would be able to connect an employee to the department it belongs.

Confusing? Don't worry just yet.

Since the primary keys are used as reference for connecting tables they can't be repeated, so it's also a good practice to make the ids auto increment themselves, meaning that you won't have to control the ids or type it, the database itself will take care of that and fill these fields for you and make sure there are no repetitions.

The rows are data inserted on the table, for instance, the rows for the table employees, would be each employee the company has.

Check the below example:

Employees Table

id	name	date_of_birth	admission_date	salary	department_id
1	Paul Lyons	1985-03-09	2015-05-12	3000	1

Departments Table

id	name
1	Finances
2	Human Resources

Thanks to department_id on the employees table, we can tell that the employee Paul Jones belongs to the department named as "Finances" and not "Human Resources". It's also possible to have a clear vision of what are columns and what are lines by looking at the above example.

Most part of the databases use a language called SQL (Structured Query Language), depending on the chosen database, there could be variations of the SQL, but the essence is basically the same. Summarizing, it doesn't matter if you choose MySQL, PostGres or even Oracle, you will need SQL. The examples here shown will be based on MySQL because it comes with the previously suggested servers.

PHPMYADMIN

If you installed any of the suggested servers in the beginning of the book, you should be able to access PHPMyAdmin by accessing the link http://localhost/phpmyadmin.

PHPMyAdmin is a database manager that allows creation of databases, tables as well as the management of the database as a whole.

The next examples will use a database called "learning". In order to create it, follow the steps:

1. Click on "new" at the left top of the screen.
2. Name it after "learning".
3. Click on Create.

See the illustration:

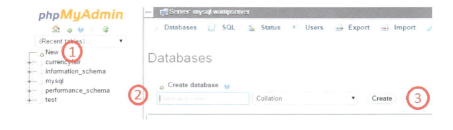

After creating the database it should appear at the list on the left side, same place as number 1 on the above image. In order to list the tables that the database contains, all you need to do is click on it. Since no table have been created, the database will be empty.

To create tables, name it and set the number of columns that it will have, for this example, 6 as shown on the following picture:

When finished, press "Go".

Now the data of all the columns that the table will contain must be set. The most important here is that differently to PHP, the data type in SQL matters. In short, a column that is ready to receive integer numbers cannot receive text or even decimal numbers. An explanation on the different SQL data types can be found at:

http://www.w3schools.com/sql/sql_datatypes_general.asp

Follow the example:

Name	Type	Length/Values	Default	Collation	Attributes	Null	Index	A_I	C...
id	INT		None			☐	PRIMARY	☑	
name	VARCHAR	100	None			☐	...	☐	
date_of_birth	DATE		None			☐	...	☐	
admission_date	DATE		None			☐	...	☐	
salary	FLOAT		None			☐	...	☐	
department_id	INT		None			☐	...	☐	

Table comments:

Storage Engine: InnoDB   Collation:

PARTITION definition:

Save

On this example, id is being used as "integer" and the A_I means auto-increment, that's needed in order to guarantee that a new id will be generated in each row and the index has "primary" selected indicating that this is the primary key.

The column "name" is a varchar (a short text field), its length (max number of characters) is set to 50.

The type for the field "salary" is set to float which allows decimal numbers.

The date_of_birth and admission_date fields are set to be of the type date.

The field department_id is set to be of the integer type.

This is a tiny introduction on databases, the least you need to know to work MySQL on PHP. About the data types, if it still confusing, my advice is that in the beginning you choose int for numbers and varchar for everything else. **Doing so will affect directly the quality of your application**, but won't bring any visible damage for small projects while you learn. Taking some time to explore PHPMyAdmin can help you improve your comprehension of databases as a whole.

CONNECTING

Connecting to a database is relatively easy on PHP. The easiest method, *in my opinion*, is the mysql_connect, however this is going to be removed over the course of the next versions due to its low security. So for the next examples, we will be using PDO to execute database operations.

The syntax for connecting to a database using PDO is as follow:

$bd = new PDO ('mysql:host=localhost; dbname=aprendizado; charset=utf8', 'root', '');

The localhost term above is to be overwritten by the location of the database, in this case since we are working in a local server, it's going to be localhost. The dbname term serves as a specifier for the database name which in this case is going to be "learning". Charset specifies the characters codification to be used, we will be using utf8 for now. The first term after the comma, root, is the username credential for the database, and the second term that is empty right now is the password credential. By standard the servers recommended will use these credentials, if it doesn't work, try using root as password and as username.

In short a database was created and PHP is now able to connect to it.

In case the syntax is looking a little weird for you, don't worry because PDO uses a concept called object orientation, which is a different model of PHP. I strongly advise the learning of the Object Oriented PHP *as soon as you have got the grips with PHP, don't worry with it just yet though, for now just memorize the syntax.*

INSERT

As seen, no SQL code was used to connect to the database, the same logic won't apply for the next examples

The SQL syntax for inserting rows on the table employees is:

INSERT INTO employees (name, salary, date_of_birth, admission_date, department_id) VALUES ('Edward', '3000', '1991-05-31', '2014-09-10', '2');

To get the above command executed on PHP, first we need to store it in a variable. Follow the example:

```php
1   <?php
2   $db = new PDO("mysql:host=localhost;
3                 dbname=learning;
4                 charset=utf8",
5                 "root",
6                 "");
7   $sql = "INSERT INTO employees
8               (name, salary, date_of_birth, admission_date, department_id)
9               VALUES
10              ('Edward', '3000', '1991-05-31', '2014-30-04', '2');"
11  $db->exec($sql);
```

On line 2 the connection with the database is established and the data for the connection is stored in the variable $db.

The SQL command is stored in the variable $sql and executed on line 11 by using the exec method.

The syntax may seem strange but you get the grips to it soon.

UPDATE

```
UPDATE employees SET name = 'Edward Johnson', salary =
'3400' WHERE id = 1;
```

The above syntax updates one (or more) rows previously inserted on the database. On the previous example, the name is being updated to "Edward Johnson" and the salary to 3500 where the id equals to 1.

DELETE

```
DELETE FROM employees WHERE id = '1';
```

The previous SQL code deletes all the rows where the employee's id on the table employee equals to 1.

EXAMPLE PROJECT

This project uses the previous example of sessions as basis. In this project, the login example will be integrated to a database, allowing users to register and login in the system.

First the file database.php has to be included on the top of the index.php file and dashboard.php, a the first lines of both files are as shown below:

```php
<?php
session_start();
include("functions.php");
include("database");
?>
```

Now the file database.php has to be created and filled with the following code:

```php
<?php
function connect(){
    $db = new PDO("mysql:host=localhost;dbname=example;charset=utf8", "root", "");
    return $db;
}
?>
```

You will also need to add a link to the register page on index.php, on the following example it is possible to see the link inserted just below the form.

```html
<form method="post">
    <p>Username: <input type="text" name="username"/></p>
    <p>Password: <input type="text" name="password"/></p>
    <p><input type="submit" value="enter"/></p>
</form>

<p>Not a member yet?
    <a href="register.php">Register now</a>
</p>
```

It's also needed to alter the function validateCredentials on the file functions.php so that the credentials can be validated based on data coming from the database.

```php
1   <?php
2   function validateCredentials( $username, $password ){
3       $db = connect();
4       $result = $db->prepare("SELECT * FROM members WHERE username=? and password=?");
5       $result->execute(array( $username, $password ));
6       $lines = $result->fetchAll( PDO::FETCH_ASSOC );
7
8       if (count( $lines ) > 0){
9           return true;
10      }else{
11          return false;
12      }
13  }
14  ?>
```

Notice on line 15, the user equals to "?" and the password to. This happens because on the method execute that is on the following line, the variables $user and $password are passed.

The code could be rewritten this way:

$query = "SELECT * FROM members WHERE user = '$usuario' AND password = '$senha'";

Easier and more direct, nevertheless when you write your code that way there is no protection against SQL Injection, a very common way of hacker attack.

The page register.php needs to be created. The code is seen next:

```php
1   <?php
2   session_start();
3   include("functions.php");
4   include("database.php");
5   ?>
6   <html>
7       <head>
8           <meta charset="UTF-8">
9           <title></title>
10      </head>
11      <body>
12          <h1>Register</h1>
13          <?php
14          if (isset( $_POST["username"] )) == true){
15              $username = $_POST["username"];
16              $password = $_POST["password"];
17
18              $db = connect();
19              $query = "INSERT INTO
20                          members
21                              (username, password)
22                          VALUES
23                              (?, ?)";
24              $result = $db->prepare($query);
25              $result = $result->execute(array( $username, $password ));
26
27              if ( $result == true ){
28                  ?>
29                  <p>
30                      You successfully registered! Click
31                      <a href="index.php">here</a> to login
32                  </p>
33                  <?php
34              }else{
35                  ?>
36                  <p>Username in use, please try again!</p>
37                  <?php
38              }
39          }else{
40              ?>
41              <form method="post">
42                  <p>Username: <input type="text" name="username" required/></p>
43                  <p>Password: <input type="password" name="password" required/></p>
44                  <p><input type="submit" value="register"/>
45              </form>
46              <?php
47          }
48          ?>
49      </body>
50  </html>
```

Similarly to login.php, first it's checked if the method post is being used, in case it is it tries to register the user, if not, shows the register page.

Notice too that there is a test validating if the user was really inserted and in this case the most probable cause for it to not be is if the username is taken. The validation used isn't the best one, but it's a start.

Now the database for the above example needs to be created. Create a database called example and a table called members with the following structure:

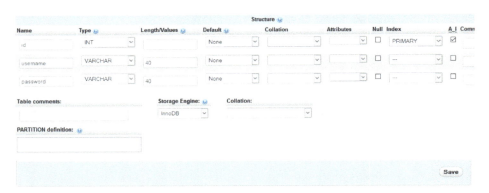

And *Congratulations! Now you should have a system that allows register, login, logout and has access permissions. You may not notice but you have learnt a lot about sessions, arrays, databases, functions and even more.*

If you still have questions on the previous example, good news, we will review everything on this example with a different approach. If you understood everything, congratulations, the next example will enforce what you've learned and will bring some new stuff.

On this example a register of cars will be created, the user will have the ability of registering cars, listing them, editing previously registered cars and delete them.

Below we have the code for the file register_1.php that contains nothing but pure and simple html, its form is pointing to a PHP page called register_2.php.

```
1   <html>
2       <head>
3           <meta charset="UTF-8">
4           <title></title>
5       </head>
6       <body>
7           <h1>Register a car</h1>
8           <form action="register_2.php" method="post">
9               <input type="text" name="model"
10                      placeholder="Please type the car model"
11                      required/>
12              <br/>
13              <textarea name="description"
14                      placeholder="Please type a detailed description of the car"
15                      required/></textarea>
16              <br/>
17              <input type="submit" value="Register"/>
18          </form>
19      </body>
20  </html>
```

And below we have the file register_2.php that gets the data filled on the form through the method post, connects to the database through a function that we will create later called connect and inserts data on the database. After the insertion verifies if the insertion really happened and shows a success message or an error message depending on the result.

```php
1   <?php
2   include("functions.php");
3   ?>
4   <html>
5       <head>
6           <title></title>
7       </head>
8       <body>
9           <h1>Register cars</h1>
10          <?php
11          $model = $_POST["model"];
12          $description = $_POST["description"];
13
14          $db = connect();
15
16          $query = "INSERT INTO
17                      cars (model, description)
18                  VALUES
19                      (?,?)";
20          $preparing = $db->prepare( $query );
21          $result = $preparing->execute(array( $model, $description ));
22          ?>
23          <?php if( $result == true ){ ?>
24              <p>The car was successfully added</p>
25          <?php }else{ ?>
26              <p>An error occurred</p>
27          <?php } ?>
28      </body>
29  </html>
```

The next example shows edit_1 which is very similar to register_1.php, the main difference is that the fields are auto filled with the data of the car to be edited.

```php
1    <?php
2    include("functions.php");
3
4    $id = $_GET["id"];
5    $db = connect();
6
7    $query = "SELECT * FROM cars WHERE id = ?";
8    $execute = $db->prepare($query);
9    $execute->execute(array( $id ));
10   $result = $execute->fetch( PDO::FETCH_ASSOC );
11   ?>
12   <html>
13       <head>
14           <title></title>
15       </head>
16       <body>
17           <h1>Edit car</h1>
18           <form action="edit_2.php" method="post">
19               <input type="hidden" name="id"
20               value="<?php echo $result["id"];?>"
21               required/>
22
23               <input type="text" name="model"
24               placeholder="Plese type the car model"
25               value="<?php echo $result["model"];?>"
26               required/>
27
28               <textarea name="description"
29               placeholder="Plese type the detailed description for the car"
30               required/><?php echo $result["model"];?></textarea>
31               <br/>
32
33               <input type="submit" value="Register"/>
34           </form>
35       </body>
36   </html>
```

The file edit_2.php works on the exact same way as register_2.php.

```php
1  <?php
2    include("functions.php");
3
4    $id = $_POST["id"];
5    $model = $_POST["model"];
6    $description = $_POST["description"];
7
8    $db = connect();
9
10   $query = "UPDATE cars SET model = ?, description = ? WHERE id = ?";
11   $execute = $db->prepare($query);
12   $execute->execute(array( $model, $description, $id ));
13
14   $result = $db->query( $query );
15
16   header("location: list.php");
17  ?>
```

Below is the delete.php file:

```php
1  <?php
2    include("functions.php");
3
4    $id = $_GET["id"];
5    $db = connect();
6
7    $query = "DELETE FROM cars WHERE id = ?";
8    $prepare = $db->prepare( $query );
9    $result = $prepare->execute(array( $id ));
10
11   header("location: list.php");
12  ?>
```

Below is the functions.php file:

```php
1  <?php
2  function connect(){
3      $db = new PDO("mysql:host=localhost;dbname=car_store;charset=utf8",
4                    "root", "");
5      return $db;
6  }
7  ?>
```

The file index.php is composed of links to other pages only.

```
1   <html>
2       <head>
3           <title></title>
4       </head>
5       <body>
6           <h1>Car Store</h1>
7           <ul>
8               <li><a href="register_1.php">Register a new car</a></li>
9               <li><a href="list.php">List cars</a></li>
10          </ul>
11      </body>
12  </html>
```

Last but not least, list.php:

```
1   <?php
2   include("functions.php");
3
4   $db = connect();
5   $query = "SELECT * FROM cars";
6   $result = $db->query( $query );
7   ?>
8   <html>
9       <head>
10          <title></title>
11      </head>
12      <body>
13          <h1>List cars</h1>
14
15          <?php if (count( $result ) == 0){ ?>
16              <p>No cars found</p>
17          <?php } else { ?>
18              <table>
19                  <tr>
20                      <th>ID</th>
21                      <th>Cars</th>
22                      <th>Description</th>
23                      <th>Actions</th>
24                  </tr>
25                  <?php foreach ( $result as $car ){ ?>
26                      <tr>
27                          <td><?php echo $car["id"]; ?></td>
28                          <td><?php echo $car["model"]; ?></td>
29                          <td><?php echo $car["description"]; ?></td>
30                          <td>
31                              <a href="edit_1.php?id=<?php echo $car["id"]; ?>">Edit</a>
32                              |
33                              <a href="delete.php?id=<?php echo $car["id"]; ?>">Delete</a>
34                          </td>
35                      </tr>
36                  <?php } ?>
37              </table>
38          <?php } ?>
39      </body>
40  </html>
```

If you got so far, congratulations, that means you have acquired all the basic knowledge for coding PHP and MySQL! I hope you learned the enough to proceed by yourself now and that your expectations on this book are met.

"Anyone who stops learning is old, whether at twenty of eighty. Anyone who keeps learning stays young. The greatest thing in life is to keep your mind young." (Henry Ford)

Keep on learning!